ATTAIN PEAK

REFEREE FITNESS

How to Train Smarter to Become a Better

Referee & Balanced Individual

BENJAMIN T. MUELLER

GU09992002

Special thanks to the past referees, instructors, assessors, coaches, and other people in the world of soccer with whom I have worked.

Thank you to Thomas Bobadilla for your foreword. It means the world to me.

Special thanks to family and friends who have continued to push me to pursue my goals and passions.

Also by Ben Mueller

ATTAIN PEAK RUNNING THROUGH CROSS-TRAINING:
How to Train Smarter to Become a Better Runner & Balanced Individual

THE OPERATING MANUAL FOR GREAT HEALTH:
How to Achieve Peak Wellness and Find Your True Self

CONTENTS

Foreword

WITH *ATTAIN PEAK Referee Fitness,* Ben Mueller provides referees, and people in general, an effective guide for keeping yourself healthy and fit. He takes an approach that makes it simple for everyone to engage in all aspects of a well-rounded training program, breaking his plan of action into three phases that are easy to understand and apply:

- ➢ Nutrition
- ➢ Training and
- ➢ Recovery

Ben has spent years leading soccer referees and learning about various training programs. He has combined his learnings with his own ideas to develop a process to help you effectively train to maintain a top fitness level and a well-balanced life.

Thomas Bobadilla
Former FIFA and MLS Assistant Referee
US Soccer National Referee Coach

Introduction

Importance of Fitness for Referees

FITNESS IS VERY important for soccer referees to consider. In professional and international soccer, the referee runs more miles than most players during the game.

Referees have to maintain excellent aerobic fitness so they can keep up with the match for the full ninety minutes or more of play. After all, being tired will affect the referee's physical positioning and mental decision-making during the game. Referees also must have the ability to sprint fast during quick counterattacks and dynamic play over the course of each game.

In addition to this, referees and assistant referees must be able to run using a variety of motions. They must be able to run backwards, sideways, and even shuffle side-to-side.

While it is true that just being fit will not make you a good soccer referee, a referee with poor fitness will never be great at their job. Good fitness is absolutely essential to being a good referee.

Another aspect referees must consider is recovery between games. With the increasing demands placed on today's referees to cover more games, recovery is becoming very important. Referees must learn strategies to recover better and get ready for the next game.

In this book, you will learn how to fuel your body for optimal on-field performance. You will learn key workouts that allow you to move around the field better. Furthermore, the book will enhance your understanding of recovery and the process by which the body gets more fit.

With that, I leave you to enjoy the book. If you have any questions, please do not hesitate to contact me at ben.mueller7@aol.com.

Bonus Tip from Ben: Always take on a growth mindset with your training. Continue to read and have conversations with others. No matter how much you learn, there is always more to learn.

Reality

HERE ARE A FEW sad realities that need to be addressed:

- ➢ More than fifty percent of adult referees go through an injury every year and are sidelined because of it.
- ➢ Many referees have weak upper-body strength and cannot complete a set of five chin-ups.
- ➢ Most referees run slower every year, despite doing similar numbers of game.
- ➢ More than forty percent of referees are not at their ideal weight for their height, despite refereeing lots of games.
- ➢ More than fifty percent of referees do no cross-training at all.

These are just a few of the startling statistics that point to a sad reality. But the good news is this sad reality can actually be changed with some adjustments, goals, and a different attitude.

That is what the ideas in this book attempt to do.

The truth is we do not necessarily have to train *harder*, but we *must* train *smarter*. We must perform quality workouts, give our body proper recovery time, and consume the right foods for faster recovery and better fuel.

That last sentence is a great summary of the key to better referee fitness and a healthier self. It is a program that I know will not only make you a better referee, but also a more balanced individual.

So, let me ask you:

> - Do you want to become a more fit referee?
> - Do you want to increase your full-body fitness?
> - Do you want to be happier and healthier than before?

➤ Do you want to feel strong and energetic day in and day out?

I believe the ideas in this book will help you get closer to your goals. Welcome aboard!

Conventional Approach to Problems

MANY REFEREES MAKE NO effort to improve their referee fitness in the off-season or during the season. Other referees believe the only way to improve their referee fitness is through running. Their limited perception tells them that running is the only way to improve referee fitness.

Another major problem is that officials are often expected to work multiple games or games on a daily basis. This can make it very difficult for referees to recover or improve their fitness. Because of this, a large number of referees suffer injuries every year.

13

General Idea

EACH REFEREE is different in terms of the number of miles he or she can safely run, how they respond to training, and how they recover from workouts.

This Attain Peak Fitness approach proposes, rather than pushing the referee to improve fitness by running more miles than their body can handle, the referee should run a comfortable number of miles and use cross-training as a way to gain more fitness than would be achieved with more running.

The cross-training should mostly be done before or after running. In some cases, the referee can alternate between running and cross-training activities, such as cycling or pool running.

For example, five minutes of running followed by five minutes of pool running, repeated six times. These workouts are referred to as combination workouts in the book.

Injuries

THE HUMAN BODY was designed to move about ten miles per day. Our ancestors had to hunt and gather food, and they moved around a lot.

Human beings are certainly not the fastest creatures, but we have possibly the best endurance of all the creatures. Our bodies were designed by evolution to move slowly for about ten miles per day through a combination of running and walking.

Despite what people tell you about bad knees, human beings were born to run. Injuries are almost always caused by a combination of muscular imbalances, poor running form, and too many miles.

Notice that I did not say improper footwear. The shoe companies would like you to believe that it is all about the shoe. But shoes are oftentimes one of the contributors to injuries. The reason for this is that shoes can alter our running strides and cause us to run in a way that is not natural. Then, over time, we develop injuries from this alteration of our form.

Not only that, but we have lots of nerve sensors on the soles of our feet. Shoes also block those nerve sensors from making contact with the ground.

I recommend most referees learn to run in shoes that are light. Light shoes have several advantages listed below:

- ✓ They allow for a fast leg turnover rate. (You want each foot to hit the ground a total of 170-200 times per minute, regardless of pace)
- ✓ They allow you to run as close to your normal form as possible.
- ✓ They allow you to run faster during races and workouts.

17

✓ They are easier to perform a natural foot strike with.

✓ Light shoes are fairly cheap in comparison to the designed shoes.

✓ Your arches and lower leg muscles become stronger over time.

Some referees who have different types of foot strikes or running form may benefit from a shoe with more cushioning or stability. That said, I would encourage everyone to get their form analyzed by an expert and then learn to run in a way that minimizes risk of injury. Strength training may be necessary to improve the strength of muscles surrounding key joints.

Injuries can be *acute* or *overuse*. *Acute* injuries are due to a sudden movement that causes a bone, muscle, or joint to move out of place. An example of an acute injury is an ankle sprain, as it is due to excessive twisting of the ankle. *Overuse* injuries occur over a long period of time. Common overuse injuries include plantar fasciitis and runner's knee.

Most running injuries are overuse injuries that can be healed fairly quickly. Depending upon the location and severity of the injury, runners can maintain fitness by cross-training more and running less. This program is especially good for injured referees, because it allows for modification in the run versus cross-training time during the combo workouts.

If a referee feels an injury coming on, they can simply perform a cross-training activity and run less. They can even deep water run, cycle, or do a combination of the two for several weeks, to maintain or even improve fitness during injuries.

To greatly decrease the chances of injury, follow these tips:

- ✓ Give your body forty-eight hours of recovery after a race or hard session.
- ✓ The day after a hard workout or game, pedal a bike easy, or do some easy deep water running to help the body recover.

✓ Spend adequate time stretching. For example, if you perform a forty-five-minute training session, spend at least fifteen minutes stretching all your muscles after.

✓ Perform a dynamic warmup prior to every workout.

✓ Get regular chiropractic care and massages to help your body recover.

✓ Look into using a foam roller before and after each workout or game.

✓ Drink enough water.

✓ Eat a wide variety of fruits, vegetables, and whole grains. The foods have antioxidants that help the body recover.

✓ Monitor your land running miles and utilize more deep-water running and cycling.

✓ Strength train your full body at least twice per week, and aim for full-body fitness.

###

Bonus tip from Ben: Soreness after a hard workout or game is a sign that your body needs to recover. Never attempt to push through pain. Always better to back off the training and heal so little injuries do not turn into major injuries.

Stress Fractures

STRESS FRACTURES ARE a referee's worst nightmare.

When a referee experiences pain or tenderness in an area, it could be a muscular injury and not a bone issue. If it is a sharp pain, however, that persists during running, the likelihood of a stress fracture increases.

Stress fractures are mainly caused by a combination of poor nutrition and too much land running. Regular combination workouts minimize the chances of a stress fracture, because they limit the land running and increase the amount of cross-training. A healthy diet that includes lots of plant-based foods and limited amounts of processed foods further reduces risk of stress fractures.

Side story

I knew a thirteen-year-old girl who was an excellent runner. She was running 5k times around twenty minutes, which is extremely fast for a girl her age. When she got to high school, her coach increased her mileage to forty miles per week, and she got a stress fracture on each shin within three weeks of the season.

With her new coach, her mileage had more than tripled what she'd been doing when she was on a combination workout program, a year earlier. Once she recovered from her stress fracture, she reduced her land running, did more combination workouts, and within a few years, her 5k time improved to nineteen minutes.

Young kids and especially young girls have a higher likelihood of stress fractures for several reasons. Their bones are still in the process of developing bone density by storing calcium. Because of this, a coach must be very careful when designing a training program for a young athlete. They must carefully monitor the "stress" load and "recovery" time of the athlete. Not doing so can be fatal!

When a referee runs, the bones actually become stronger through the osteoblasts that occur each time the foot strikes the terrain. Running is as good for your skeletal system as it is for your muscular and cardiovascular systems. The problem arises when the demands and stress of an referee's training come faster than the referee can recover. That is why the referee must space out the land runs accordingly, so the full body including the skeletal system can recover. If the skeletal system gets adequate recovery, the bones will bounce back even stronger, just like the muscles and the rest of the body systems.

Nutrition also plays a key factor in preventing stress fractures. In particular, calcium and vitamin D are critical. Adequate vitamin D levels can be taken from the sunlight. Vitamin D works with other vitamins and enzymes to get calcium to the bones. During the colder months, it is a good idea for a runner to consider a vitamin D supplement. The recommendation by many holistic health doctors for vitamin D3 is at least 400 international units per day. Besides keeping your bones strong, vitamin D also plays a significant role in preventing other diseases.

###

Bonus tip from Ben: Stress fractures can mostly be avoided by monitoring your training and taking time to recover.

Program Overview

YOUR TRAINING PROGRAM is an interaction between three phases

1. Nutrition
2. Training, and
3. Recovery

The idea is that each one of these three phases is equally important. If you want to get the full benefit of training, you must take each of the three phases seriously.

For example, you will not build fitness by stressing out your body constantly without taking time to recover. Further, if your diet consists of the Wisconsin food pyramid (beer, bratwurst, and cheese), your workouts will suffer. If you want to get excellent results, you cannot slack on training, recovery, and nutrition.

Discipline is a key ingredient for achieving success, especially in running. Without a doubt, if you want to reach your full potential as a referee, you must take the three-phase program—nutrition, training, and recovery—seriously.

The recovery phase is important because, without the recovery of all of your body systems, you will not become a better runner. Remember: your body actually gets stronger during the recovery phase. Ample recovery time is crucial for gaining fitness benefits.

The training phase consists of the workouts, the cross-training, strength training, and core work. The recovery phase consists of stretching, time off between workouts, massages, chiropractic care, and other things that promote all your body systems to recover. The nutrition phase consists of the foods you eat to fuel your body and allow for optimal recovery.

The nutrition and recovery phases intersect in that what you eat can affect your recovery. There are certain pro-recovery foods and anti-recovery foods that we will get into in the nutrition section. Again, the underlying essential idea is that your training performance is the interaction between the three phases.

I have always believed the idea that you can be as successful as you want to be. That said, you cannot escape from the consequences of your choices. Your success ultimately depends on the choices you make. Performing combination workouts, healthy eating, and even promoting recovery takes dedication.

You will be doing less land running, but your training volume will go up. For example, a regular program might call for a six-mile run. Instead you could create a similar workout by doing deep water running intervals for forty-five minutes, then run two miles at an intense pace on land, then cool down with some more deep water running. Thus, your land running mileage will be less, but your overall training volume will be greater. You will also have to stretch before and after the workout, as well as strength train and do core work regularly.

This is by no means an easy program and will require more time and dedication than a regular "just run" program.

Bonus tip from Ben: Recovery must be looked at as PART of the training process. To improve your fitness, you must take recovery just as serious as the tough workouts.

Low Mileage

THE SIMPLE IDEA behind training is to stress the body, allow the body time to recover, and then, as a result, the new fitness level is built. That is stress, recover, and adapt! A referee actually gains more fitness during the recovery phase and achieves the maximum benefit after they are fully recovered.

One of the biggest mistakes referees make is overloading the body again before it is fully recovered. The consequences of this are detrimental and will cause a referee not to reap the maximum benefits from their workouts.

Your body is very smart. It has a built-in healing mechanism that allows it to recover in a timely manner after a workout. Not only that, but the body will bounce back stronger after a rigorous workout to better prepare itself for next time.

For example, a long-distance runner actually builds more capillaries through endurance training to better assist the body in delivering oxygen to the muscles. Oxygen delivery and carbon dioxide removal are critical for allowing the body to run long distances, such as in marathon training. Another example is that a weight trainer's muscle cells get bigger as a result of intense weight training.

Once your body has fully recovered, you are now ready to do another intense quality workout to gain more fitness. The key is performing that intense workout after you are fully recovered, but not waiting too long after. There is a window of time called the "super compensation window" in which you have to complete the next workout in order to add on to previous fitness gains. If you wait too long, your fitness level will drop and your fitness gains will not be as high.

A good rule of thumb is that you have about three days after you are fully recovered to perform the next intense workout in order to add on to those gains. Of course, that number can change depending upon the individual, prior history, the activity, and other factors.

During the recovery phase, you can perform slow and easy exercises. For example, you could go for an easy run on a recovery day or pedal a dual stationary bicycle easy. This is actually beneficial, because it removes some of the lactic acid out of your body and helps re-energize the muscles by increasing blood flow. The key is not to work out fast, hard, or intensely, as that will interfere with recovery.

Lifting weights and strength training are also generally a bad idea on a recovery day for obvious reasons. It is actually better to lift immediately following a hard or fast aerobic workout and then allow the muscles time to recover.

If you have taken any physical fitness class, you have probably heard of the terms overload, progression, and specificity. *Overload* refers to putting more demand and stress on the body than comfortable. *Progression* refers to gradually increasing the amount of stress over time. *Specificity* refers to selecting a specific area of fitness or muscle group to improve prior to designing a workout.

Bonus tip from Ben: Every workout you do should always have a purpose. The great running coach Jack Daniels says, if you do not know the purpose of the workout, you should go home and watch television. Same is true for referees!

Stress All Body Systems

WHEN YOU RUN, you are placing stress on all of the body systems. Many people fail to recognize this. Fitness experts call long distance running a form of cardiorespiratory exercise, because it engages the heart and lungs. The respiratory system must take in oxygen from the environment, send that oxygen to the blood stream, and then the blood stream delivers the oxygen to the cells.

The training involved in running will not only involve the cardiovascular and the respiratory systems, but also the skeletal, muscular, endocrine, digestive, and nervous systems. The nervous system is the system that controls all of the other body systems by sending messages (known as neurons) throughout your body.

Combination workouts should be designed to engage all of the body systems appropriately. For example, when you deep water run, the skeletal system gets a break while the other systems are hard at work. By strength training, you better prepare your muscular system for the demands of running. Cross-training such as swimming and cycling allows a runner to work their cardiovascular and respiratory systems while giving their skeletal system a break. Impact exercises such as land running help strengthen the skeletal system by creating osteoblasts inside of the bones and developing greater bone density.

###

Bonus tip from Ben: When starting a new cross-training activity, start gradual and easy. As you get more experienced with the activity, then feel free to challenge yourself more with it.

Recover All Body Systems

THE KEY THING to remember when recovering is that all of the body systems need to recover. This includes the bones, muscles, cardiovascular, respiratory, endocrine, and nervous systems.

Running places a large demand on all of these body systems, and because of this, these systems need to be given time to recover. If these systems are allowed to recover appropriately, the body then will bounce back stronger than before. On the other hand, if adequate recovery is not allowed, then the body can gradually break down and become weaker.

When we experience muscle soreness and physical pain, it is a sign that our muscular and skeletal systems need to recover. The last system to recover completely is the nervous system. This is because the nervous system is the command center of the body and is responsible for leading the recovery process.

The following are great tips to recover properly:

- ✓ Leave at least forty-eight hours between hard games and hard workouts.
- ✓ Run on a variety of surfaces and do at least half of your running on soft surfaces.
- ✓ After a workout, consume super-foods that are high in antioxidants, carbohydrates, and proteins.
- ✓ Use a foam roller to massage all of your large muscles including your back.
- ✓ Consider getting a deep tissue massage periodically.
- ✓ Stretch all of your large muscles after a workout.
- ✓ Consider using compression socks as a way to relieve leg soreness.

✓ The day after a game or hard workout, pedal a stationary bicycle easy or do a light deep-water running session to increase blood circulation.

Bonus tip from Ben: Recovery days are my favorite. After a hard workout or game, I enjoy going for a nice, easy bike ride, doing yoga, and foam rolling.

Quality versus Quantity Training

BEFORE STARTING ANY workout, the referee should ask the question: "What is the purpose of the workout?"

The famous running coach Jack Daniels states, if an athlete cannot answer that question, then they should go home and watch television.

After all, all workouts should have a purpose. The purpose might be to recover, build speed, or improve stamina.

Just running for the sake of running and adding more miles is not a purpose. If one wants to improve and get better, then one must plan each workout skill fully, so their body gets the best benefit from the workout.

Most traditional running programs have referees running lots of miles every day. This training program calls for three quality workouts every training cycle (about ten days). The three quality workouts are the tempo, intervals, and long workout.

###

Bonus tip from Ben: I typically plan workouts in ten-day cycles. I try to get a long workout, interval workout, and tempo workout each training cycle. Sometimes, I need to adjust the workouts based on how I feel.

Tempo Workout

A TEMPO WORKOUT consists of a warmup, then intense activity, and a cool down. You can think of it as a moderate to intense workout sandwiched between an easy warmup and cool down.

The lengths of your tempo workout will depend on your training goals. The program also allows you to get creative with the type of activity you do during the tempo workout.

Some examples of great tempo combo workouts are below.

- 10 minutes easy cycling, 15 minutes of running at 10k pace, 10 minutes easy cycling

- 10 minutes easy running, 20 minutes moderate pace on dual stationary bike, 10 minutes easy running
- 10 minutes easy pool running, 20 minutes moderate pace pool running, 10 minutes easy running

The goal is that the middle portion of the tempo run should be a good pace, but not so fast that you are breathing heavy. For referees, think about your pace if your running medium effort during a game.

Bonus tip from Ben: By running hard in the water and easy on land, you can give your legs a break from the pounding and train your legs to turn over quickly.

Long Workout

ONE TIME IN EVERY training cycle, you should complete a long workout. The goal of the long workout is to get your body systems used to moving for a long time.

You can utilize a combination of activities to complete the long workout. For example, you could run for thirty minutes, ride a dual stationary bike for thirty minutes, and then swim laps for an hour.

In general, the long workout should be about two hours. This will give the referee added fitness for a 90-minute game or longer.

The pace of your long workout should be easy and controlled. You do not want to be breathing heavy until the very end of the workout. Again, the key parts of the long workout are length of time and controlled pace.

Bonus tip from Ben: By doing a variety of activities during your long workout, the time will go much faster.

High Intensity Interval Training (HIIT) Workout

ONE TIME DURING every training cycle, you should alternate between bursts of speed and easy recovery. This workout best simulates an intense soccer game.

The total distance of the fast intervals should add up to two to three miles, but you may begin a training program with less total interval distance. When doing high-intensity interval training, the recovery time, interval intensity, and interval length all factor into the stress of the workout. I recommend doing an active recovery, where you are at least walking during the recovery interval. Keep in mind your intervals can include swimming, cycling, rowing, elliptical, pool running, or any mixture of them.

Some examples of great High Intensity Interval Training combo workouts are below:

- Pedal stationary bike easy for ten minutes, run at a hard pace 400 meters, followed by two minutes of walking recovery (repeat six times), swim easy for ten minutes.
- Pool run easy for ten minutes, run at a medium intense pace for one minute followed by ninety-second walking recovery (repeat eight times), swim easy for ten minutes
- Run easy for eight minutes, run all-out for thirty seconds followed by one-minute active recovery (repeat ten times), bike easy ten minutes

###

Bonus tip from Ben: Part of the benefit from HIIT comes from forcing yourself to run fast while you are fatigued. Make sure that your recovery period is active and does not involve just standing still.

Summary of the Three Quality Workouts

A TEMPO WORKOUT is fast training sandwiched between an easy warmup and cool down. Depending upon the referee's ability level, the tempo workout can be anywhere between twenty to sixty minutes.

An example of a tempo workout is:

- ✓ 10 minutes of easy pool running
- ✓ 10 minutes hard pool running
- ✓ 10 minutes hard land running
- ✓ 10 minutes easy cool down of pool running

A LONG WORKOUT is where the referee builds endurance. The rule of thumb is that your long workout should be at least as long as your game, but preferably longer (it could go into extra-time).

An example of a long workout is:

- ✓ 20 minutes easy cycling
- ✓ 20 minutes easy pool running
- ✓ 20 minutes easy land running
- ✓ 20 minutes easy pool running

A HIGH INTENSITY INTERVAL TRAINING (HIIT) workout is quick bursts of speed followed by longer periods of recovery. For example, you might pedal a bike as fast as you can for thirty seconds and then pedal the bike super-easy for two minutes. An example of a high-intensity interval training workout is:

- ✓ 10 minutes of easy cycling
- ✓ 30 seconds all out cycling followed by 2 minutes of easy cycling (15 repeats)
- ✓ 10 minutes easy land running

These workouts are not done only by land running, but by combining land running with either deep water running or cycling.

For example, a forty-minute tempo run could be changed to twenty minutes of land running and thirty minutes of deep water running.

The other days each week are spent recovering between the workouts and usually consist of either pure rest or a combination of easy cycling, land running, and deep water running.

The idea with the other workouts is to get the lactic acid out of the muscles and help the body recover. The total number of miles spent land running is usually under twenty miles for stronger runners and fifteen miles for others.

The program never calls for more than one workout per day. The body needs a full twenty-four hours to recover and, in the case of intense workouts, forty-eight hours.

Two-a-day workouts force the body to work out when it is in the process of recovering and for your average runner do more damage than good. It is critical to take it easy the day after a quality work out and give both your fast twitch and slow twitch muscles time to recover.

Bonus tip from Ben: I have found that planning is key. Spend at least fifteen minutes each week planning your workout schedule for that week.

Year-Round Fitness

ONE OF THE GREATEST aspects of doing combination workouts is that it promotes year-round fitness. Many referees on this program work out year-round and, as the exercise volume increases, are ready to jump into a competitive game at any point of the year.

This is not true of traditional training programs! In traditional training programs, referees usually go through a periodization phase and then greatly reduce mileage during the off-seasons. When the next season starts, traditional training programs have referees run a lot of base mileage (usually for ten weeks or more), then do quality intense workouts, and finally taper off prior to the race.

After the main season, traditional training programs usually have referees greatly reduce mileage, causing the athlete to lose fitness. Then, when the next season starts, athletes go through the cycle again.

I see this all time with young high school runners. The cross-country season runs from late August to early November. Usually in October, the high school runners are running their best and by January most high school runners are not in condition to race. This constant cycle of training hard and then starting over is not ideal.

With the combination workout approach, athletes/referees maintain excellent fitness year-round and do not go through these cycles. The reason is simple! The combination workouts allow the athletes/referees to train at a high intensity all year without the risk of burnout. Besides this, the cross-training activities can also change throughout the year making it more enjoyable mentally.

If a referee wants to build on their fitness level and run faster, this can be done at any point during the year.

The referee needs to increase the overall training volume or intensity of the workouts.

Keep in mind that with combination workouts, referees are almost always running less than twenty miles per week, so their muscular and skeletal systems will not need to take the large break during the year that traditional programs take. An athlete also has the option of decreasing the running mileage and increasing the deep water running or dual stationary cycling mileage. This is one of the many great aspects about this program, as it allows for more flexibility.

Because of the fact that referees are alternating between different types of exercises, the chance of burnout decreases greatly. Then, if the referee wants, they can officiate games on the spur of the moment and make that decision at any time.

###

Bonus tip from Ben: To keep yourself motivated throughout the year, consider entering a variety of 5k or 10k running races.

Base Training and Quality Training

THE THREE BASIC training periods are base building, quality period, and then the taper period. The exact amount of time spent in each period varies between athletes and desired race distances. Combination workouts can be utilized in all three training phases.

Typically, before a referee can engage in quality workouts, they must complete a sufficient amount of base training. The base training period can be anywhere from three to twelve weeks depending upon the desired race distance.

During the base training period, the referee should do a lot of easy runs followed by some time spent cross-training. The cross-training time does not need to be super-intense but should involve some time working out at a moderate pace.

For example, an referee could run two miles and then jump in the pool and do thirty minutes of moderate pool running.

Once the base training period is over, then the referee can begin adding the quality workouts discussed before, tapering down days or weeks prior to the season.

All Types of Referees – Youth to Professional

THE GREAT THING about combination workouts is they can be effective for all levels of referees. They can prepare novice referees for their first youth game and help stronger referees perform better, and help an experienced referee keep up with the pros. Personally, I find combination workouts to be challenging, fun, and rewarding, and they help enhance recovery.

Today, I run only about twenty land miles per week, and I find myself outrunning most of the players during the games that I referee. My favorite aspect of the program is that keeps me in great shape year-round and allows me to referee strong at any given point during the year.

The key to this program is quality intense aerobic training, strengthening the muscles involved in training, and adapting the body to the running motion.

Bonus tip from Ben: Fitness is not lost as fast as people tend to believe. If a fit referee took a few weeks off of running, they would lose a little fitness but would bounce back quickly after running again.

Synergistic Effect

WHEN YOU COMPLETE high-intensity combination workouts, take time to recover, practice recovery techniques, and put high-quality food in your body, your body begins to get the benefits of all the phases. This synergistic effect cannot be underemphasized and is the key to quality running.

Many people tell me things such as the following:

- ➢ They want to do the combination workouts, but do not want to take time to stretch.
- ➢ They will follow the training aspects of the program, but they're going to stick to their beer and pizza diet.

> ➤ They will do the training workouts but cannot possibly take time to recover between workouts.

The problem is, when you eliminate parts of the program, you lose the synergistic effect. The training, stretching, combination workouts, strength training, plant-based foods, and recovery all have a positive effect on your body when included together. If you eliminate one of these, you begin to lose this synergistic effect, and the quality of training drops.

This effect only happens when everything is followed as closely as possible. Sure, there are times when you might get off track a little, but the key is to get back on track right away.

Throughout the years, the program has been modified based on experiences with different training approaches. If someone suggests something and it works well with the program, then I add it as part of the program. On the other hand, I throw it out if it does not work well with the program.

For example, I found that weight lifting programs that demand lots of intensity in a short amount of time can backfire and increase risk of injury. At first, I thought this would be a good supplementation, but I found it interfered with recovery and increased injury risk. Instead, I have had greater success with weight lifting that is controlled, focuses more on form, and involves more repetitions and less weight.

You may receive a lot of backlash from others when you tell them about more cross-training and less running. Just a fair warning! Some will tell you that you are crazy for thinking you can run fast by running less and spending more time cross-training. Many simply will dismiss this without giving it a chance, either because it is a newer idea to them or there's some closed-mindedness.

Training Progression

WHEN YOU WORK OUT, your body believes you are working out for survival. For all your body knows, you are running away from a tiger or lifting a heavy rock for survival. Because of that, your body adapts to the stress and prepares itself better for the next fitness endeavor.

Your body is very smart and adapts to the stress that it is put on. Progression is a key principal to improving fitness. Fitness improves when the body is challenged. If the body is challenged too much, then injury can result. The goal is basically to push your body slightly past its comfort zone and then recover, so your body can adapt to its new level.

Thus, it is very important for the referee to slowly build on their level of fitness. It is also critical that athletes take periodic breaks from heavy training to allow their bodies time to recover.

Bonus tip from Ben: The "innate intelligence" of the body is what allows the body to become more fit as a result of stress. But it is really all about the idea of "stress, recover, adapt." The body does not get stronger until it has fully recovered.

Training Volume

THE TRAINING VOLUME refers to the entire load of training. This includes the running, cycling, swimming, pool running distances, and any other cross-training that you are performing. It does not matter if the workout distance was easy, medium, or hard, as it all goes into your training volume.

The great part of this program is you can increase your training volume through cross-training while putting less stress on your muscular and skeletal systems. Recovery is still critical, and the body must be given adequate time to recover between workouts, or you will not reap the benefits of the increased training volume.

65

It is also important to note that increasing volume is not the only way to improve total body fitness. Listed below are several other options that you have:

- ➢ Increase the intensity or speed at which the workout is performed.
- ➢ Take less recovery time between intervals during an interval run.
- ➢ Increase the distance of a quality workout and then take an extra recovery day.

Bonus tip from Ben: Continue to look for new ways to challenge your body and always try to keep it guessing.

Stressing the Body System

WHEN YOU TRAIN, all of the body systems are stressed in some way. All of the body systems must recover and get restored back to full health. This is why good nutrition, adequate water intake, sleep, stretching, massage, chiropractic care, and all the other parts essential for optimal recovery are critical. The idea is we train, stress the body systems out, and then let all the body systems return to full strength.

The human body is very smart, as it has a built-in healing mechanism that allows the body to recover completely from disease and breakdown. For example, if you cut yourself, the body eventually heals and recovers. And if you catch the flu, your body eventually defeats the virus and you restore back to full strength.

When you stress your body through rigorous training and allow your body complete recovery, the body eventually recovers. Not only that, but your body bounces back even stronger than it was prior to the rigorous workout. This is the innate intelligence of your body at work, as it realizes it needs to better prepare itself for the next challenge.

Intensity versus Quantity

THE ISSUE OF intensity versus quantity is always an interesting debate in the fitness industry. A simple example is this: would a runner be better off running five miles slowly or two miles at a fast pace?

Of course, the answer may vary per individual athlete and is based on the desired race distance training for.

When I was a child, I swam on the swim team, and I could never understand why we swam five miles per day when my desired race distance was only fifty yards. I began to question if the time would be better spent working on stroke technique as opposed to completing lap after lap.

My personal belief is that the athlete should focus on intensity more than total volume. The athlete can perform well without ever completing runs more than double their desired race distance.

The great thing about the human body is it will adapt to whatever type of stress you put on it. If you lift a lot of heavy weights, you will turn into a power lifter. If you run regularly, your body will turn into a runner. If you sit on the couch regularly and live a sedentary lifestyle, then you will turn into a couch potato.

When you put your body through an intense workout, the body builds itself and prepares for the next workout by becoming more fit. A great example of this is that, through exercise, your body builds new capillaries, allowing for more efficient oxygen delivery. This happens in much the same way as when our body fights to rid ourselves of viruses when we get sick. Not only does the body get rid of the virus, it remembers the virus to better prepare itself to fight the virus next time it comes. It is your body's innate intelligence at work!

Proportional Training

ONE OF THE BIGGEST problems with traditional training program for referees is there is a disproportionate amount of running, strength training, and cross-training.

For example, many referees will go out and run a lot of miles per week and only spend a few hours cross-training and strength training. I have talked to many high-level referees who tell me they strength train and cross-train, but when you look at the actual amount of time they spend strength training, it is very minimal compared to their time spent running.

I am a firm believer that a good portion of the training time should be spent strength training, core training, and developing flexibility. The referee should also spend a great deal of the training time cross-training.

The following are a few of the many risks and dangers to following a training program of the typical referee (85% running, 5% cross-training, 5% strength training, and 5% flexibility):

- ✓ High chance of mental burnout and loss of vigor
- ✓ Poor muscle balance and lack of full-body strength
- ✓ High chance of serious injuries such as stress fractures
- ✓ Potential long-term damage of ligaments and joints
- ✓ Higher chance of overtraining

Another major problem that usually happens when a referee's training is not in the ideal proportion is overtraining. Overtraining is a major problem in both high school and college athletes.

It has been said that a referee is better ten percent *undertrained* than just one percent *over-trained*. This is very true!

The following are signs and symptoms of overtraining:

- ✓ Change in mood and attitude
- ✓ When the referee feels that they need more sleep than usual to recover
- ✓ When the athlete experiences an overall feeling of fatigue
- ✓ Not enjoying activities that the referee once enjoyed
- ✓ Changes of menstrual cycle for females
- ✓ When the muscles feel tired and sore
- ✓ When the referee no longer looks forward to their workouts

###

Bonus tip from Ben: If you are no longer looking forward to your workouts, that is a sign you may be becoming mentally stale. It may be time to back off or switch your training up a bit.

Super-Compensation Window

IT IS IMPORTANT to understand the idea of stress, recovery, and adaption. The general idea is we stress our bodies by completing a workout, then we recover from that workout, and our body adapts to that level of fitness.

Let's say, for example, a couch potato begins to walk for thirty minutes and completes this workout five times each week. Since the couch potato went from no exercise to exercising regularly, they are going to see huge fitness gains within a few weeks. Then, after the fitness gains, if they do not work out any harder, they are not going to see any more improvements. They are just going to be able to maintain their current fitness.

I know lots of runners and referees who just continue to do what they have always done and never see any improvement as a result. If we want to improve, we must increase the stress on our bodies progressively.

The super-compensation window is important for all referees and trainers to understand. Understanding this concept is crucial to developing fitness and becoming a more fit referee.

First, our bodies get stronger during the recovery phase. That means, when we work out, we do not reap the benefits of that workout until our body is fully recovered, which is why it is important to take time and let the body recover after a hard workout or race.

After the body is done recovering, you will have reached a new level of fitness. You then have a window of time to complete another intense workout and increase fitness even more.

The key factor is to make the next intense workout more intense than the previous one. This can be done in the following ways:

> ➤ Shortening the recovery times, if doing intervals or repeats.
> ➤ Simply run a longer distance or longer distances during intervals.
> ➤ Attempt to run the repeats or intervals at a faster pace for the same amount of time or distance.

Like all windows of time, the super-compensation window will only last for a few days, and if an intense workout is not completed in that time, the body will lose the ability to build on the previous intense workout. Because of this, it is critical that an athlete listen to their body and complete intense workouts after recovery has occurred, but not wait so long that the super-compensation window ends.

In this program, we can aim to get better constantly or just during specific periods of a training season. For example, a referee might aim to improve their fitness only around their season and just look to maintain fitness the rest of the year.

Personally, for myself, I prefer to build my fitness regularly and take a few weeks off, if I feel worn down mentally or physically. What I have noticed throughout the years is I rarely feel burned out with this program, though, due to the constant variation it provides.

Combo Workouts

COMBINATION WORKOUTS are one of the key aspects of the training program. Basically, they allow you to build your aerobic capacity while reducing the stress on your overall body.

Since the running motion is important to master and your body must get used to running, it is a good idea to run a few miles on land and then follow it up with some cross-training. For example, you could warm up on an elliptical machine then run two miles on land, and then jump back on the elliptical for more intense training. This gets your aerobic system used to moving for a long period of time and reduces the pounding that your joints take from running.

I prefer to use the dual stationary bicycle and pool running as my main cross-training activities, but you can also choose another that matches your interest.

###

Bonus tip from Ben: The dual stationary bicycle is one of the best fitness machines ever invented. Consider purchasing a dual stationary bicycle. Any running workout can be simulated on it.

Strength Training

(Builds Capillaries; Improves Aerobic Capacity)

TO RUN EFFICIENTLY, overall body strength is very important.

Every muscle in the body, from the facial muscles down to the feet, is used during the running motion. The muscles that surround the feet must be strong, to help your feet support your full body weight. The muscles around your legs must be strong to perform their duties as shock absorbers and propel you forward. The upper-body muscles must be strong to keep your posture upright and allow maximum oxygen consumption to enter your lungs during running.

Many referees ignore strengthening their upper bodies, which creates muscle imbalances throughout the body.

When it comes to strength training, this program emphasizes exercises that use your own body weight. These exercises should be performed roughly three times per week, post-run. I have found it is best to perform these exercises after running on days in which you are not recovering.

Start out in the beginning stage for each exercise, and work your way to the next stage once you feel ready.

Exercise	Stage 1	Stage 2	Stage 3
Front plank:	30 secs	1 min	2 mins
Side Plank:	15 secs	30 secs	1 min
Calve raises:	15 reps	30 reps	60 reps
Leg kicks:	15/leg	30/leg	60/leg
Wall sits:	30 secs	1 min	2 mins
Pushups:	15 reps	30 reps	60 reps
Dip:	20 reps	40 reps	80 reps
Superman:	30 secs	1 min	2 mins

Core strength

A LARGE PART of your energy in running comes from your core. The core consists of your abdominal muscles, back muscles, the muscles around the buttocks, and the muscles around the hips. Running speed and efficiency comes from a combination of a strong core and proper running form.

Not only this, but your core muscles also help stabilize the foundation of your skeletal system, which is your spine. Because of this, a strong core can result in a more balanced running form and reduced likelihood of injury.

While running alone will help strengthen the core muscles, it is beneficial for runners to perform various core exercises regularly, to gain additional core strength. The following exercises should be supplemented into the fitness program to improve core strength:

> **Front plank**: The front plank is a great isometric exercise that engages all of the core muscles. All referees should work their way up to holding the front plank comfortably for four minutes. (It can be done!)

> **Side plank:** The side plank is a great isometric exercise that engages the stubborn muscles on the sides of the body.

> **Reverse crunch**: This is a great exercise that works the lower abdominal muscles. Work your way up to two minutes' worth of reverse crunches.

> **Bicycle crunch:** This is a great exercise that works the upper abdominal muscles and oblique abdominal muscles. Work your way up to two minutes' worth of bicycle crunches.

➢ **Superman**: This is a great isometric exercise that works the back and hip muscles. Work your way up to holding the superman pose for two minutes.

➢ **Weight training:** Weight training is a great way to engage the core in a variety of ways. Just make sure not to overdo the weight and always allow proper recovery time between sessions.

➢ **Yoga:** Yoga is a great exercise that forces your core to remain engaged throughout each pose. Yoga is a great supplement to a running program.

➢ **Core workout videos:** There are a variety of ten-minute core workouts that engage your core muscles in a variety of ways. Search your local bookstore or fitness store for some workout videos.

###

Bonus tip from Ben: Try to do the core and strength training exercises at least twice per week. You can do them after a workout or on an off day.

Pool Running

RECENTLY, I WAS deep water running at my local YMCA, and a good friend of mine asked me if I was injured. He had assumed that, because I was taking time to deep water run and cross-train, I must have an injury preventing me from pounding the miles.

Once I informed my buddy that I deep water run several times per week, he was very surprised. Unfortunately, this "cross-train only if you have to" mentality is a common belief amongst many referees and athletes. Mainstream running coaches often only use deep water running and other forms of cross-training on their runners if they are injured. It is as if these people are a slave to the idea that we should run tons of miles when we are healthy and then cross-train only once we get injured.

Deep water running takes practice, but it is very easy and surprisingly fun, once you get the hang of it. First of all, you need to perform deep water running in deep water and preferably with a depth of at least one foot larger than your height. Then you need to wear a flotation belt that allows you to maintain an upright position when in the water. Many aquatic centers have flotation belts you can use, or you can purchase your own for about fifty dollars. The flotation belt goes around your waist and allows you to maintain an upright position while in the water.

Then once in the water, you simply mimic the running motion as close as you possibly can. It does take practice to get the hang of it! Keep the following tips in mind when performing deep water running:

> Have a slight forward lean, like you would while land running.

- Turn your legs over similar to the way you would while running.
- You should find yourself slowly moving forward. It is easiest when you can find some space that is open (at least fifteen yards). Your best bet is to utilize the deep end of your own lane in a pool.
- Utilize short strides and try to increase your cadence (leg turnover rate) to around 100-130 strides per minute.
- To get your heart rate up, you will need to perform intervals while deep water running. You can simulate a track workout based on the perceived time it would take you to complete an interval distance.
- To simulate hill running, you can purchase special types of water-running shoes that add resistance to your feet.
- You can perform deep water running on a recovery day by just running at an easy pace for a period of forty-five to sixty minutes.

➢ Deep water running can be done as part of a combination workout to increase the volume of a workout and decrease the pounding of your joints, bones, and muscles. For example, you could run for three miles easy and then do deep water running intervals for thirty minutes.

Deep water running is a great cross-training tool that referees can use before or after a run to gain more training volume. I typically will deep water run after I log in a few miles of land running, as a way to lengthen my workout, increase my aerobic capacity, and improve my leg turnover rate.

Because the water is much thicker than air (roughly 500 times thicker), one will not be able to maintain as fast as a cadence when deep water running. A good cadence to attempt to maintain is around 120 leg turnovers per minute (sixty revolutions per foot).

Keep in mind that a good running cadence when land running is roughly 180 leg turnovers per minute.

###

Bonus tip from Ben: In the water, your heartrate will not be as high as on land. The key to pool running is leg-turnover rate. Try to maintain a leg turnover rate of 60 times per minute.

Dual Stationary Bicycle

A DUAL STATIONARY bicycle works both your arms and your legs. These bikes were very popular in the 1980s and can often be seen at hospitals for rehabilitating patients.

They are the bikes with the large flywheel, and they work off of your own resistance. i.e., the resistance increases as you pedal and move the bike faster.

Today's fitness centers have moved away from these training devices, so oftentimes they are not available at gyms, which is unfortunate, because dual stationary bicycles are one of the most efficient training tools that exist.

My parents had one in their basement, and I worked out on it quite a bit as a teenager. The bike was called an Air Dyne, and I would simulate running workouts such as intervals, tempo runs, long runs, and speed workouts regularly. Once, when I was injured, I trained on the Air Dyne for eight straight weeks and ran a great two-mile race.

I calculated it out that a dual stationary bicycle can give you seventy-five percent of a running workout in the same period of time you could spend running. That means, if you want to simulate a thirty-minute run, you would need to spend about forty minutes on the dual stationary bicycle.

The dual stationary bicycle works great with this training program, as it allows for a great cardio-respiratory workout and develops muscle strength in the legs and arms. I recommend utilizing the dual stationary bicycle roughly two times per week and creating combination workouts that involve land running with the dual stationary bicycle.

Cycling

REGULAR CYCLING is also a great cross-training activity for referees. Both mountain biking and road biking provide a great opportunity to cross-train, build aerobic fitness, strengthen leg muscles, and be outdoors.

The big difference between cycling and the other exercises mentioned is that cycling is stationary for the upper body. Because of this, I believe the dual stationary bike is still a better cross-training activity than traditional cycling for referees.

On the other hand, outdoor cycling gets you outside and can serve as a great recovery workout the day following an intense workout or game. Also, mountain biking provides an opportunity to attack hills and really build some lower body strength.

Just remember to ride a bike that is fitted properly for you and have fun!

###

Bonus tip from Ben: Cycling can be a fun activity to do in the summer, but always wear a helmet. Also, try to choose a route that is free from traffic.

Swimming

SWIMMING IS A great exercise to build aerobic fitness while giving your body a break from the pounding. I have known several runners to spend hours in the pool each week while reducing the lengths of their running sessions. The have found that their running improves.

Besides lap swimming, you can also tread water and get a great cardio session in that way. Usually, when I do pool workouts, I do a combination of pool running, treading water, and lap swimming. I also enjoy open water swimming in the summer.

Swimming is a great exercise to maintain and even improve fitness during injuries or when your body just needs a break from the pounding.

###

Bonus tip from Ben: I like to alternate between 100 yards of swimming and three minutes of pool running. I usually swim the 100 yards at a decent pace and then pool run easy.

Rowing

A ROWING MACHINE is a great way to increase your upper-body stamina and get a cardiovascular benefit at the same time.

For maximum benefit, learn the proper form for rowing. Rowing can improve core, arm, and back strength.

Shoes

WHEN IT COMES to shoes to train in, the shoe experts like to run around claiming their shoe is the best option for runners. Shoe companies have done a great job using propaganda techniques to attract runners and triathletes to their shoes, and most of their shoes cost over $100.

Running shoe stores and so-called shoe experts attempt to convince runners that injuries can be prevented by wearing the right shoe. While I agree that the wrong shoe can contribute to injury, I think that muscle strength, good running form, and good recovery make a bigger difference.

Shoes alter the way we would naturally stride, cut off circulation in the feet, and also block the millions of nerve receptors in the foot from absorbing direct contact with the ground. The best shoes to wear are a pair of lightweight shoes that allow you to run in the most natural way possible.

Typically, injuries are the result of too much land running, poor overall body strength, and lack of efficient running form. Shoe choices contribute to your running form. That said, the best shoes for runners vary on an individual basis, based on foot type and running gait.

Nutrition: Eat for Health

THE FOODS WE consume not only affect our fitness but also our overall health. There is a strong link between the foods we consume, our fitness levels , and performance in life in general.

Today we see many kids diagnosed with ADHD, obesity, and diabetes. Without a doubt, this is affecting our kids' performance in all areas of life. We should seek to improve our diets, not only so we run better, but also so we increase our health and longevity.

As Charlotte Gerson states, our bodies have a natural healing mechanism, and we must nourish our bodies with the right balance of nutrients to function to our full potential.

In the developed nations, it is no secret that obesity is a common disease. Industry tells us that obesity is the result of consuming too many calories, but the problem is much deeper than that. Contrary to popular belief, obesity is actually a sign of consuming too many low-nutrient-dense foods and not enough high-quality, nutrient-dense foods.

All the processed foods we consume are depleted of nutrients because the foods are no longer in their whole form. Then, we eat the processed foods, which are deficient in a wide range of nutrients that are originally in those foods in their whole form. As a result, people are malnourished and get hungry. So, they eat more processed food, which gives them calories but does not fill the nutrient gap that they are missing.

The key to beating obesity is not to focus on calories, like industry has us believing, but to eat a wide range of whole foods in their most natural state. These foods are your plant-based foods, such as fruits, vegetables, nuts, seeds, and whole grains. Plant-based foods contain fiber, keeping us feeling full and satisfied, and giving us a wide range of nutrients.

###

Bonus tip from Ben: Consider reading the book *Spark* by Dr. John Ratey. He discusses the amazing benefits of physical activity on the brain. All the more reason to run!

Water

IT IS A POPULAR belief that everyone needs sixty-four ounces of water daily. A better rule of thumb to use is to take your weight in pounds and divide it in half. The result is how many ounces of water your body needs daily. For example, a 200-pound man needs 100 ounces of water daily.

Hydration is also vital before, during, and after working out or refereeing. During the workout, your body uses water and minerals (electrolytes) to keep your body in check. A good rule of thumb is to drink two glasses of water at least one hour prior to working out and then an additional glass of water every twenty minutes during the workout or game. If the weather is more humid, then you need to drink even more water.

Sports drinks are a great option if you are working out for longer than one hour, as they also replenish minerals. Coconut water is known as nature's perfect sports drink and provides your body with the key minerals in the right amount that your body needs. I would choose coconut water over popular sports drinks. One sports drink that I have found to be valuable is called Sustain (from Melaleuca), as it is made without the toxic food dyes that are used in most sports drinks.

Always read the ingredients on the labels of anything you eat or drink.

Bonus tip from Ben: Start each day with drinking at least twenty ounces of water upon waking up.

Organic Food

ORGANIC FOOD HAS many benefits over conventional. By definition, organic food is free from pesticides, sprays, and other chemicals. This is a big plus, because then our bodies just get the nutrients, vitamins, and enzymes from the plant and not any added chemicals.

Not only this, but organic food also has a wider variety of nutrients and vitamins due to the fact that it is grown in soil that is enriched with a wider variety of nutrients.

Another benefit of eating organic food is you do not need to worry about the plant coming from a genetically modified seed (GMO). With the increasing concern over the health problems that erupt from genetically modified crops, it is a good idea to avoid them, if possible.

It is my opinion that organic and plant-based are the best foods. It does not need to be perfect, but one should consume a wide variety of fruits and vegetables.

Natural versus Man-made

IN GENERAL, the closer a food is to its natural state, the healthier it is for us.

When food is processed, excess sugar and fat are usually added, and other bad chemicals are also put into the food. Not only this, but processing food also damages and takes away many of the healthy nutrients that were originally in the food.

That does not mean that we cannot enjoy an occasional treat every now and then, but the vast majority of our diet should be clean and natural foods.

Plant-based Foods – Synergistic Effect

MY TRAINING PROGRAM advocates for a plant-based diet. As a rule of thumb, we should limit processed foods and animal proteins (meat, eggs, and dairy). That is, we should consume primarily vegetables, fruits, legumes, and whole grains.

Further, we should consume a wide variety of plant based foods to ensure we get all the essential vitamins, minerals, and enzymes that our body needs to function as a whole. I always tell people to think in terms of color. So try to eat a wide variety of colors, including the dark green, red, and orange vegetables.

The benefit of consuming plant-based foods is they have a relatively low glycemic index in comparison to processed foods, have lots of fiber, and also are more efficiently stored by the muscles and liver as energy, as compared to high-sugar processed foods.

Colin Campbell conducted a study called the China Study that concluded humans eating mostly plant-based foods have fewer diseases such as heart disease and cancer. Campbell concluded this was primarily due to the synergistic effect that occurs in the body when we eat a wide variety of plant-based foods.

Basically, all the vitamins and enzymes in plant-based foods work together to keep us healthy in a way no doctor or nutritionist could ever explain. Each vitamin, mineral, and enzyme in plant-based foods has an effect on the others that allows the entire body to remain healthy in a synergistic way.

Not only that, but plant-based foods also are loaded with antioxidants that help fight free-radical damage, again, and disease. As a rule of thumb, everyone including runners should eat a wide variety of mostly plant-based foods such as fruit and vegetables. For more information on nutrition, the program recommends watching the documentary *Forks over Knives*, which does a full overview of Campbell's China Study.

One of the effects of capitalism is that industry will always use its own criticism to its advantage. We see this a lot in the food industry! For example, "low fat," "low carbohydrates," "high in omega 3," and the newest, "no high fructose corn syrup."

In his book, *The China Study*, Campbell argues, if one consumes a plant-based diet, there is no need to worry about targeting specific nutrients. The reason is you will get the synergistic effect of the many nutrients and enzymes that are in the plant-based foods.

Proteins

PROTEINS ARE AN important nutrient because they help damaged muscle tissue repair. This is extremely important for referees and athletes as they recover from intense workouts.

It is important to understand that all plant-based foods have some protein and, if you eat a wide variety of plant-based foods, you can meet all your protein needs.

The following are some excellent sources of proteins that will help your body recover better after workouts.

- Nuts, seeds, and beans
- Wild salmon

- Black bean burgers
- Greek yogurt

Bonus tip from Ben: Black bean soup is an excellent protein source and very tasty.

Carbohydrates

AS A REFEREE, carbohydrates are your primary source of fuel. An important nutritional concept to understand is that all carbohydrates turn into sugar, which is utilized by your muscles and cells for energy. When you exercise, your body breaks down stored sugar in your muscles and liver known as glycogen.

Foods that serve as the best carbohydrate energy sources for the body are the whole foods with plenty of fiber in them. Fruits, vegetables, and whole grains are your best sources of fuel, as they are easy on the digestive system and can store in your muscles and liver to be utilized as long-term energy.

Good choices include all fruits and vegetables, whole grain cereal, rice, pasta, and bread. When you are finished with a workout, you want to replace lost carbohydrates with simple sugars that immediately enter the blood stream. Great choices of post-workout foods include fruit juice and fresh berry smoothies.

###

Bonus tip from Ben: We probably do not need as many carbohydrates as we think we do. Try to get your carbs mostly from fruits, veggies, and whole grains.

Fats

HEALTHY FATS CAN be excellent sources of energy. Besides that, they can be great for your health, as they have good cholesterol, which can improve your overall health.

In general, excellent protein sources are also excellent sources of fat. The following are all good sources of fat:

- Almonds and cashews
- Other nuts and seeds
- Wild salmon
- Avocados
- Greek yogurt

Vitamins and Minerals

ATHLETES AND REFEREES NEED to recover at the cellular level after a workout. To do this, the referee needs to consume lots of nutrient-rich foods. Plant-based foods are very nutrient rich and contain lots of vitamins and minerals that will help your body repair from a workout or game.

I suggest consuming freshly pressed juice or fruit smoothies as a way to recover. The nutrients will get absorbed into your bloodstream quicker from juices than smoothies, but both are a great way to recover. Green juice or berry juice makes excellent recovery drinks, and you can throw in some flax seeds for extra protein and omega 3 fatty acids.

As an athlete, it is extra important to consume a wide variety of fruits and vegetables during the day. I also encourage taking a whole-food supplement such as Juice Plus as a way to ensure you are getting all the vitamins and minerals you need.

Food Toxins

RECENTLY, I WAS debating the dangers of fast food with a young mother. She told me she did not see harm in feeding her four-year-old daughter fast food, because her daughter was skinny and did not seem to store any body fat.

Unfortunately, I believe this is the stance that many young mothers take due to lack of quality nutrition education. I informed her it is not just the fat, calories, sodium, and sugar that we have to worry about, but also all of the toxins and chemicals that get put into many processed foods.

The truth is many of the chemicals that are put into processed foods in the United States are banned in other countries. The two big rules I preach to every referee and person with respect to nutrition are to limit their animal proteins and limit processed foods. Basically, eat a wide variety of whole foods that are in their most natural form.

Because industry has brainwashed consumers into thinking nutrition is all about calories, diet drinks have become very popular in our culture. The artificial sweeteners found in diet drinks and low-calorie foods are not healthy. Everyone needs to know that artificial sweeteners trick the digestive system into thinking it is getting real sugar and consequently cause consumers of diet beverages to crave refined grains (hence junk food) long term. Not only this, but these artificial sweeteners have undesirable consequences. Stevia is a natural, low/no-calorie sweetener that is one of the best ones to use as an alternative.

Diet beverages are *not* a health drink. They can contribute to weight gain and drinking them can have serious side effects.

###

Bonus tip from Ben: There are a variety of local natural grocers and online shopping stores that carry an assortment of non-toxic or less toxic products.

Supplements

AS HUMAN BEINGS, it is critical we get all the vitamins, minerals, and enzymes in the right amount. This is why we want to consume foods in their natural whole form and not processed foods that have been depleted of nutrients.

As referees, we need even more nutrients than sedentary people. Vitamins, minerals, and enzymes play a key role in keeping our bodies healthy and allowing our bodies to recover from the stress of running. The following is a list of nutrients that all referees should consider for optimal health and recovery. Of course, one should discuss this with their medical doctor first.

- ✓ **Vitamin D.** Vitamin D is also known as the sunshine vitamin. It is actually more of a hormone than a vitamin. It regulates thousands of different functions in the body. Many studies support that high levels of vitamin D in the blood are effective in preventing diseases including cancer.

- ✓ **Probiotics.** The human digestive tract has good bacteria that help food get absorbed and digested.

- ✓ **Omega 3.** Current research supports that most Americans are too low in omega 3 fatty acids and too high in omega 6 fatty acids. It is optimal for us to have a ratio closer to three omega 6s to one omega 3; the ratio for most Americans is around 15 to 1. Good sources of omega 3 include flax seed, fish oil, and coconut oil.

- ✓ **Plant nutrients**. Consuming a variety of brightly colored fruits and vegetables is essential for optimal health and recovery. I prefer a product called Juice Plus that consists of live plant material from over forty different fruits and vegetables.

###

Bonus tip from Ben: Consider getting your blood checked annually to check for vitamin and mineral levels.

Carbo Loading

CARBOHYDRATES AND FATS are the referee's primary source of energy during refereeing and workouts. Because of this, referees should consume a diet that consists of mostly carbohydrates and healthy fats. The idea is to get your carbohydrates through whole foods as opposed to refined processed carbohydrates. Good sources of carbohydrates include whole grains, vegetables, and fruits.

The idea of carbohydrate loading is really only relevant if you are running a marathon distance or longer. Since our games last under two hours, you should fuel your body with mostly carbohydrates in the days before the game, but you do not need to overdo it. Just stick to your regular eating plan, which should consist of eating meals of mostly whole grains, fruits, and vegetables.

Calories

THE OBESITY EPIDEMIC in America is caused by people consuming more calories than their body burns. The energy balance equation states that if a person consumes more calories than their body burns, they will gain weight. If they burn off more calories than they consume, then they will lose weight. Finally, if they consume the same amount as they burn, they will maintain their weight.

Even the most conservative dietitian would agree it is typically safe to consume 250 calories less than your body burns, if you are trying to lose weight. The problem begins when an athlete cuts calories by too much. Cutting calories can lead to eating disorders and other health problems in athletes.

A major concern in women's athletics is the female athlete triad, which is when female athletes show the three symptoms of amenorrhea, osteoporosis, and disordered eating.

Referees and other athletes need to consume enough calories to satisfy their training demands. The average human burns around 2500 calories per day, but runners burn calories in addition to this when they run or work out. For example, a 150-pound runner burns roughly 150 calories per mile run. Cross-training and strength training activities burn calories too, and should be factored into the referee's caloric needs.

My recommendation is not that referees count calories, but that they make sure they're eating enough nutrient-dense foods that provide an adequate amount of calories for their energy needs. Consuming lots of whole, plant-based foods such as fruits and vegetables are an easy way to make sure you do not over eat. Plant-based foods have lots of fiber, which makes a person feel full and helps the nutrients digest easier.

I tell referees their goal should be to consume ten different servings of organic fruits and vegetables every day. My belief is, if people focused more on the *quality* of foods they consume and less on the *calories*, they would be more successful with their nutrition goals.

Bonus tip from Ben: Even though I do not advise counting calories, it is a good idea to know how many calories your body burns per day. There are plenty of online calculators that can help you with that.

Recovery Foods

GOOD NUTRITION can do wonders to help aid recovery. Within thirty minutes of a workout or game, it is a good idea to consume something with simple sugars and protein.

Throughout the day, you want to replace lost nutrients with high-quality fruits, vegetables, nuts, and seeds. Drinking plenty of water is also great for helping your body recover to its full extent.

Foods that are high in refined sugars make it more difficult for the body to recover and can prevent your body from full recovery. Also, consider supplements such as vitamin D, omega 3 (from fish oil or plant based), and whole foods.

Recovery/Nutrition link

IF YOU EAT poorly, performing well as a referee will be much more difficult.

To illustrate with an example, assume a super-fit referee shows up to a game still hung-over from a night of drinking. On the other hand, a less-fit referee shows up to the game after getting a good night sleep.

There is a chance the less-fit referee will out-perform the super-fit referee just because of behavior the night before the game

The same holds true for nutrition. By eating well and getting enough rest, you can assure yourself of performing the best your training will allow you to.

No doubt, just eating healthy and sleeping will not make you a great referee. But it can be said that without good nutrition and rest, you'll never reach your full potential.

Ketogenic Diet

EVERY CELL IN the body needs glucose for fuel. Glucose is a sugar that comes from carbohydrate foods. If the cells do not get their preferred source of fuel, they can use fat and protein for fuel. This metabolic state is called ketosis.

The ketogenic diet has recently gained a lot of popularity amongst both regular people and athletes. The idea behind this diet is to get the body to burn mostly fat and protein as fuel.

I have heard mixed reviews of this diet from different experts. Colin Campbell, the author of *The China Study*, believes that a high-protein and high-fat diet increases the risk of various diseases. Many people have had success losing weight on this diet and the most likely reason for this is they get away from eating high sugary processed foods.

As mentioned earlier, I mostly support a diet of lots of plant-based foods and whole grains. If one eats a nutrient-dense diet and limits processed foods, they should have the energy they need for high-level running and refereeing.

Flexibility

FLEXIBILITY IS VERY important for a number of reasons. A flexible referee is less likely to get injured, will create speed easier, and will recover from workouts better. Because of this, it is important for all referees to work on flexibility on a regular basis.

Flexibility can be improved through dynamic and static motion stretches. The key areas of flexibility are calves, hamstrings, quadriceps, hip flexors, and back. One of the best ways to improve flexibility in these areas is to practice yoga on a regular basis.

Learn a few basic yoga poses and perform them for ten minutes at the end of a workout. Over time, you should see your flexibility improve. It is also a great idea to learn some basic static stretches and perform them at the end of a workout, too. I discuss some ideas and options in the next few sections.

Bonus tip from Ben: Consider doing yoga a few times per week. Even fifteen minutes of yoga can help with recovery.

Dynamic Stretch

DYNAMIC STRETCHING is simply stretches that involve movement of the targeted muscle. The goal is to gradually stretch the targeted muscle through movement.

Dynamic stretching is the type of stretching that should be done before every workout and game. Besides getting the muscle ready for activity, dynamic stretching also creates a better connection between your nervous system and muscles.

Examples of great dynamic stretches to do prior to a workout include:

- butt kicks
- high knees

- side steps
- lunges
- calf raises
- back twists
- jumping jacks
- arm circles and
- leg swings

Bonus tip from Ben: When on a road trip, consider stopping every hour or so and doing these dynamic stretches. They can prevent stiffness later on.

Static Stretch

STATIC STRETCHING is a great way to improve your range of motion. Increasing your range of motion will decrease your chance of injury and make you a faster runner and referee.

The best time to static stretch is after a workout is complete. You want to make sure to hold each stretch for at least thirty seconds and progress into the stretch gently.

The science behind improving flexibility is the same as improving other areas of fitness. You must overload the muscle you are trying to stretch and progressively increase your range of motion. You should never stretch to the point of pain or severe discomfort, however.

Gentle static stretching is also a great way to help your body recover in the days following a challenging workout or race. Make sure to stretch out your calves, hamstrings, lower back, hip flexors, and quadriceps.

Bonus tip from Ben: Your muscles will stretch best following a workout. That is the time to work on flexibility.

Stretching Time

MY RECOMMENDATION is that a referee spends a good amount of time stretching before and after a workout and game.

For example, if the referee completed a sixty-minute workout of running and biking, then they should spend about twenty minutes static stretching after the workout and about ten minutes performing dynamic stretches prior to the workout. The dynamic workout prior to running should usually last around ten minutes and the static stretching component after the workout should last longer for longer workouts.

Under no circumstance should the referee cut their stretching time short. This is oftentimes something that runners who are following traditional programs will do, if they are running low on time. If you do, you are asking for an injury.

Not only that, but improving one's flexibility also makes them faster and able to more efficiently exert their fast-twitch muscle fibers. All referees and athletes need to constantly strive not only to maintain, but to improve their flexibility.

Pain-Killers and Anti-Inflammatory Medications

UNFORTUNATELY, MANY referees and athletes resort to medications to push through pain. This is a bad idea for many reasons.

There are lots of studies to support that regular use of ant-inflammatory and narcotic drugs increases the risk of injury and further damage to the body. Prescription narcotics block pain receptors that communicate to the body that something is wrong. At the same time, narcotics do nothing to help the body heal or improve health.

Furthermore, narcotic medications are very dangerous and can lead to addiction and liver damage.

It is my opinion that a referee who relies on over-the-counter or prescription medication to get through workouts should take time off or back away from their training. I take a very strong stance against both narcotic pain killers and ant-inflammatory medications.

The following are excellent ways to improve recovery and promote healing that do not involve drugs:

- ➢ Chiropractic care
- ➢ Massage therapy
- ➢ Foam rolling
- ➢ Pain relief creams (Biofreeze, Icy Hot, etc.)
- ➢ Ice
- ➢ Heat

Massage Therapy

MASSAGE THERAPY has its advantages when it comes to recovery and relaxation of muscles. A massage will get the blood and lymphatic fluid flowing through your body, allowing for better detoxification and recovery.

If you can afford it, a weekly massage is a great idea. You can also use foam rollers, massage rollers, and other tools to give yourself a massage. I personally use a foam roller and a running tool called "the Stick" almost every day pre- and post-workout.

Chiropractic Care

CHIROPRACTIC CARE is a great addition to your recovery program. Contrary to popular belief, chiropractors do a lot more than make your back feel better. Chiropractors adjust your spine, which is the foundation of your skeletal system.

Your spine runs all the way from the base of your brain to your tailbone. When the three curves of your spine are in the optimal positions, your skeletal system is better able to absorb the shock of running, so you will be able to run with more efficiency and your overall body will be balanced, decreasing the chance of injury.

When it comes to chiropractors, they are all over the board on what they claim they can do. Find a chiropractor who understands fitness and is willing to listen to your concerns. A good chiropractor should examine your spine based on an x-ray, explain to you the results of your x-ray, and offer their plan on correcting problem areas.

A lot of world-class athletes see a chiropractor several times a week. It is my recommendation that serious runners see a chiropractor on a weekly basis. This allows for optimal recovery and health for the runner.

Just a fair warning, though: many of your friends will discourage you from visiting chiropractors. Chiropractors have gotten bad-mouthed over the years for being quacks and just wanting your money. Nothing could be further from the truth! They attempt to heal the skeletal system and human body using natural methods and without drugs. Many people who visit a chiropractor regularly find themselves feeling more energetic, getting sick less, and just feeling better overall.

Bonus tip from Ben: If you see a chiropractor, do not be afraid to ask questions and learn about the science behind chiropractic care.

Foam Rolling

FOAM ROLLING is a great way to help boost the recovery of your muscular system and, also, enhance the performance of your nervous system during a workout or game.

Get yourself a large foam roller and roll all of your lower-extremity muscles several times each week post-workout. I believe in foam rolling prior to static stretching as a way to prepare large muscles for activity and enhance recovery.

Make sure to roll each of the major muscle groups of the legs—the hamstrings, calves, quadriceps, and also the lower back.

If you have never foamed rolled before, it may be quite painful at first, but after a while, the muscles adapt.

Towel Stretching

STRETCHING WITH A towel can be a great way to get more out of your stretching sessions. You can use the towel to get a better stretch of your calves, hamstrings, quadriceps, shoulders, back, and arms.

Most collegiate and elite athletes use similar stretching techniques, using a rope, before and after running.

Slowly work on improving your flexibility over time, and you will notice fewer injuries and less soreness and stiffness with your fitness program.

Rest Time

MAKE SURE TO take adequate time between workouts to rest. After a hard game, I always take at least two days and do light recovery workouts.

Recovery workouts allow your muscles to recover and adapt to the rigorous workout or game. Recovery workouts can also boost your immune and cardiovascular systems.

Recovery workouts can be anywhere from thirty to sixty minutes. The following make great recovery exercises, and you can perform a combination of them during your recovery session: water running, cycling, easy swimming, walking, rowing, and elliptical.

Fast-Twitch versus Slow-Twitch

IN REFEREEING, both the fast-twitch and slow-twitch muscle fibers are used. It is critical for referees to train and develop both types of muscle fibers.

Slow-twitch muscle fibers are developed through running longer distances and moving at a slower pace. Fast-twitch fibers are developed through doing speed work, intervals, sprints, weight training, and performing anaerobic activities.

In your typical game, both fast-twitch and slow-twitch muscle fibers are used. As the speed increases, more fast-twitch and less slow-twitch fibers are used.

Lactic Acid

WHILE EXERCISING, your muscles will get fatigued in part due to the lactic acid buildup in the muscles. Through proper training and recovery, you can slow down the lactic acid buildup in your muscles.

Longer runs train your body to build less lactic acid over time, and you can then run longer without feeling fatigued. Besides this, longer runs build capillaries in your body, which leads to better oxygen absorption and less lactic acid buildup.

Basically, the body responds to training by making your body more efficient at storing oxygen and not lactic acid to your muscles.

Days Post-Game

IN THE DAYS following a game, it is a good idea to do slow and easy workouts to allow your body systems to recover completely. A good rule of thumb is to take two recovery days after an intense game.

This does not mean that you do nothing for a week, but just back off from the fast, intense training.

If you are getting adequate sleep and following a good nutrition plan, then your body will bounce back and recover quicker. The following are some good tips to follow during the days after a hard game:

> Get some extra sleep. Go to bed early and sleep until you feel fully rested.

➤ Eat plenty of fruits, vegetables, and healthy fats (cashews, almonds, and other nuts). I prefer a berry smoothie with flax seed and hemp seed for the extra protein.

➤ Take time to stretch dynamically and statically in the days following a game.

➤ Do a slow and easy workout the day after a game. I prefer to ride a bike very easy for thirty minutes or deep water run very easy for twenty minutes. Then go through a long stretching session.

➤ Do not do any weight training, as that will prevent your muscles from full recovery.

Adjusting: Listen to Body

THERE IS AN OLD saying that a referee performs better ten percent under-trained than just one percent over-trained.

Listening to your body is critical for any referee. As a referee, your body will communicate with you when it needs more rest, it feels good, and something has gone wrong. The signs that you are over-training are both physical and mental.

Adjusting your training is a necessary part of any training program. It is always best to lean on the side of caution. If you feel you need a rest or an easy day, then take it.

The following are signs that you are over-trained and may need to take a few rest days:

➤ General overall feeling of fatigue even hours after your workout.

➤ Depression, irritability, or major mood changes.

➤ Mentally not looking forward to the next workout on a constant basis.

➤ Not having the energy to complete regular routine tasks.

Gear

THE GEAR YOU USE while running and exercising is really a matter of personal preference. You want to dress in a way that you feel comfortable moving, being seen by others, and participating in your activity.

It is a good idea for referees engaged in a fitness program to invest in a decent watch, hat, sunglasses, shorts, and shirts. Over time, you will learn what equipment works well for you and what does not.

You also want to invest in a few good pairs of shoes based on your preference, foot type, and the terrain you plan to run on. Experiment with different gear to get an idea of what you like, and also discuss gear with other athletes.

Building Connections/Feedback

MEETING OTHER referees gives you a greater network of people to reach out to for support and advice. Not only that, but you can meet others who have goals similar to yours and then help one another reach those goals.

Part of being a good referee is reflecting on game performance and receiving constructive feedback from fellow referees. The more feedback you receive, the more data you have to improve your game. Working with a variety of referees will provide you the opportunity to get a variety of perspectives on officiating.

Winter

I GREW UP in the state of Wisconsin near Green Bay. The winters in northern Wisconsin are absolutely brutal and can make winter training very difficult.

Being the fearless runner that I was in my teens, I ventured outside and tackled the elements almost every day. If you do venture outside, wear a stocking hat, warm pair of gloves, and warm socks. On the real cold days, mittens are more effective than gloves at keeping your hands warm. You may also want to consider hand warmers on these days. Your body is likely to lose heat from your head, hands, and feet.

Also, dress in layers and consider wearing a pair of running tights. If the roads are slippery, a pair of tracks or spikes on your shoes can help you maintain decent traction.

Finally, there is absolutely nothing wrong with indoor training. Many days, it is much wiser to run on a treadmill and avoid slipping on ice. If you are uncomfortable with the weather, simply train indoors.

Successful training can be done indoors during the winter months.

Bonus tip from Ben: Winter running can be fun and make you feel tough. Do not be afraid to go on a treadmill on a slick day, though. Many elite runners do regular workouts on treadmills.

Humidity

THE DRENCHING HOT and humid days of summer can also pose a challenge. On these days, it is best to carry water with you during your workouts, preferably either in a light water bottle that is easy to hang on to while running or wear a fuel belt.

Also, drink lots of water before and after your run. Hydration is especially important in the summer to avoid the dangers of heat exhaustion and heat stroke.

Checking the color of your urine is a great way to tell if you are hydrated. Your urine color should be light yellow or clear. Urine that is dark yellow is a sign of dehydration, and urine that is clear is a sign of over-hydration.

It is also wise to wear sunscreen and a hat to avoid damage by the dangerous UV rays of the sun.

Consider running in the early morning or late evening hours to catch the cooler part of the day. It is usually wise to check the hourly forecast, to see when the coolest part of the day will be.

Bonus tip from Ben: Running in the early morning will give you cooler and more pleasant temps in the summer. If you have to race in the heat, you may want to acclimate your body to it prior to race day. Gradually increase time working out in the heat, and make sure to stay well hydrated.

Growth Mindset

I FIRST BECAME licensed as a USSF soccer referee at age eighteen. I had refereed recreational soccer for about five years prior to that. Needless to say, at that age, I had the fearless attitude I could handle pretty much any game or refereeing situation.

When I got the call from a tournament assignor asking if I was available to referee 18-year-old soccer games, I didn't hesitate. Not only did I take the games, but I told them I was willing to center them.

I remember showing up and thinking I was in full control of everything. But the match started, and after about three minutes, I already had major problems. It quickly it became very apparent to everyone there, including the assistant referees, players, coaches, and spectators, that I did not know what I was doing.

In that match, I had given out several cards and had to break up a fight (which you should never do). When the shortened game was over, I was so tired, I was more than ready to go home.

As an age thirty-something referee now, I am much more selective of the games I take. I only agree to take games I know I can do a great job in.

That said, I think sometimes there is an advantage to putting ourselves out there slightly past our comfort zone, so we can learn and grow as officials.

The following are some tips and guidelines that should help you with this:

- ✓ Your assistant referees make all the difference. If you're going to take games slightly past your comfort zone, make sure you have a good pair of assistant referees on that match.

- ✓ If you are injured or sick, do not be afraid to discuss switching games with the assignor. Most assignors will appreciate your honesty.
- ✓ Ask a successful referee if they would be willing to have some games with you. You learn a lot by working with a more experienced referee.
- ✓ Constantly reflect on your matches, and ask yourself what you did well and what you will do better next time.
- ✓ Find the right balance between fear and courage when selecting teams you want to officiate. Don't be afraid to accept a challenging match, but at the same time, don't get in a match that's over your head

Not Overdoing It

THE AMOUNT OF SOCCER games being played in the United States and world continues to increase every year. Unfortunately, the number of referees does not! Parental abuse and lack of time are two of the many reasons why the amount of soccer referees is going down.

Because of this, referees are expected to do more and more games. They're asked to cover back-to-back games, referee more than six games at tournaments, and referee consecutive weekdays. These are just a few of the many challenges that today's referees in soccer face.

The best piece of advice I can give you is the following. The soccer referee shortage is not your fault, and you should not have to jeopardize your physical or mental health because of it. I truly mean that! I have known many referees who feel it is their duty to officiate as many games as possible, in order to ensure all the games that need to be covered are officiated.

Every referee needs to make sure they do not overdo it. The following are signs that you may be doing too many games:

> You do not look forward to games with the same passion you once did.

> You feel physically tired and cannot keep up with play as well as you used to. (Also, may be a sign of old age... *Kidding!*)

> You notice that lingering injuries pop up more frequently.

> You find yourself reflecting less on the games and you care less about the quality of job you are doing.

You should not be refereeing every day of the week, and you should not be overworking yourself on any given day. Do not be afraid to say no or to say you need to take some recovery time.

Tournaments

REFEREEING IN TOURNAMENTS can provide referees an opportunity to gain more experience and make lots of money. Usually, tournament games are shorter in duration, and they pay the referees well for those shorter games.

Another advantage of tournaments is you get to work with and watch a lot of referees over the course of a tournament weekend. This provides newer referees a great opportunity to learn and grow their skills.

As a college student, I worked a tournament almost every weekend in the summer, and I know these tournaments really fine-tuned my referee skills. Many of these tournaments had assessors present, so I also benefited from the free developmental assessments.

That said, proper planning and preparation for tournaments is vital for a successful weekend outing. The following is a list of tips that should be considered before officiating in a tournament.

- ✓ Since most tournaments occur in the summer and require you to be on your feet for a long part of the day, acclimate your body to the heat and workload prior to coming to the tournament. A few weeks before the tournament, start by running/walking outside for up to ninety minutes of non-stop movement.

- ✓ Check the forecast and be prepared for the weather. When you sign up to referee, you never know what weather you're going to get. You will be expected to be out there regardless.

✓ When you fill out the application, be honest about the age group and amount of games you can handle. Always lean on the side of caution. When working tournaments, it is often a good idea to take games at age groups lower than where you feel comfortable. The reason for this is, since you will be doing more games, you may likely feel more tired physically and mentally after tournament refereeing than regular season games.

✓ Bring several pairs of referee socks, as there is nothing worse than refereeing in wet socks.

✓ Make sure to drink enough water. Drink twenty ounces of water before heading out to the fields and at least eight ounces of water after every half (or thirty minutes). Consider packing a low-sugar sports drink to replace minerals you may lose during the games, as well.

✓ Get as much sleep as you possibly can in the days and nights prior to the tournament.

- ✓ Sunday is always the toughest day. Your legs will be tired from Saturday, you will be mentally tired from Saturday, and you will be expected to referee the knockout-stage matches. Resist the urge to stay up too late on Saturday night, and limit the amount of alcohol you drink, if you do go out.

- ✓ Do make an appearance at the referee party, if there is one, but don't stay too long. It's fun to catch up with referees and share stories from the day, but remember: you have your work cut out for you the next day. You will need as much sleep as you possibly can get that night.

- ✓ Nutrition during the tournament is always tough. You want to eat to maintain your energy throughout the day but, at the same time, not eat too much to get an upset stomach. Great high-energy snacks to pack include nuts, peanut butter, granola bars, fruit snacks, energy gels, and trail mix.

- ✓ Even though you'll probably be provided a free meal, don't overeat at lunch. You will be more tired, if you do, and will have a harder time getting around the field afterward.
- ✓ Have fun. Maintain a positive attitude throughout the tournament. And be willing to learn and grow from others.

Summary

❖ **Full concentration:** To be successful with this training program, it requires total concentration. You must focus on the science behind the training and have an understanding of the recovery process between workouts. You must also focus on eating mostly healthy, clean, and nourishing foods that will help your body recover and prepare for the next workout.

❖ **Dedication** is the component that will be vital to your success. You must be willing to put in the time necessary to perform the combination workouts, stretching, and recovering. Lack of personal accountability and responsibility will be what separates people who cannot perform well versus those who achieve success.

❖ **Temptations:** Without a doubt, you will face temptations, at times, to skip your workouts, slack off on your nutrition, skip stretching, or just fall off your regular routine. It is important that you get yourself back on track as soon as possible. The following tips should help you stay on track and reach your fitness potential.

  ✓ **Change the time** of your workouts. Do some morning workouts, some afternoon workouts, and some evening workouts.

  ✓ **Change the location** of your workouts and try new routes. Also, train on a variety of surfaces such as trails, limestone, asphalt, sand, and a track surface.

  ✓ **Pack healthy snacks** for yourself when traveling or away from home for a long period of time. Good options include fresh fruit, nuts, and raw vegetables.

❖ **Stick to a consistent sleep schedule**. It is okay to sleep in once in a while, but try to go to bed and get up around the same time each day.

❖ **Do some workouts with other people and some solo.** Always working out by your self provides time for self-reflection but can also get boring at times.

❖ **Always allow time for pre-workout dynamic stretching and post-workout static stretching**.

❖ Always **consider trying different activities**. For example, find a local yoga or meditation class.

❖ **Do not take running too seriously**. After all, it is supposed to be fun. If you have a bad race or workout, learn from it and move on to the next one.

❖ **Blog about your running experiences or keep a journal.** Writing about running can help keep you enthused about it.

- ❖ **Visualize yourself being successful**. Create an affirmation for yourself and repeat it to yourself daily. Part of achieving success in fitness is visualizing yourself being successful.

What Now

BEN IS AVAILABLE to do speaking engagements. Invite him to talk to your referee organization, about applying the principles mentioned in this book.

Please feel free to contact Ben via email here: Ben.Mueller7@aol.com. He can do presentations that vary from one hour to four hours, and each presentation can be tailored to meet your group's needs and interests.

Recommendations

Movies: The following films are recommended to learn more about nutrition, training, and recovery:

- ✓ *Forks Over Knives*
- ✓ *Hungry for Change*
- ✓ *Fresh the Movie*
- ✓ *Food Matters*

Books:
- ✓ *Daniels' Running Formula* by Jack Daniels
- ✓ *Howard Webb: The Man In The Middle*
- ✓ *Run Less Run Faster* by Ray Moss, Bill Piece, Scott Murr
- ✓ *The China Study* by T. Colin Campbell

- ✓ *50/50 Secrets Learned by Running 50 Marathons in 50 days* by Dean Karnazes
- ✓ *Healing, the Gerson Way* by Charlotte Gerson with Beata Bishop

About Ben

BENJAMIN T. MUELLER IS a USSF soccer referee, referee coach, and referee instructor. Outside of the soccer world, he is an endurance athlete, teacher, speaker, and activist. He has taught high school and junior college mathematics and health for over fifteen years.

Since he completed his first referee course at the age of sixteen, Ben has not looked back. He has officiated over 2,000 soccer games, from youth to adult amateur level. He qualified and competed in the United States national triathlon championships three times. He is also a Badger State Games (Wisconsin Olympics) gold medalist for multiple years in both the open and master's categories.

Ben was born in Sheboygan, Wisconsin and went to college at UW-Whitewater. He earned his bachelor's degree in mathematics education and a master's degree in educational leadership at Concordia-Chicago. Currently, he is a doctoral student for education at Concordia-Chicago, doing his doctoral research on exercise and its effects on coping with math anxiety.

When Ben is not training, he can be found refereeing soccer, rooting on the Wisconsin sports teams, or relaxing in a coffee shop.

Contact Ben here: Ben.mueller7@aol.com

Or find him here: BenjaminTMueller.webs.com

Printed in Great Britain
by Amazon

72994693R00113